LISTENING TO MOTHER NATURE IN WEST VIRGINIA

LISTENING
TO MOTHER NATURE
IN WEST VIRGINIA

Poems by Ken Crawford

For information, address Anjali Crawford, Publisher:
anjalic@earthlink.net —or— ajctravels@yahoo.com

Book design and production by Anjali Online.
Distributed by Anjali Online.

First Edition: July 2005

Library of Congress Cataloging-in-Publication Data
Crawford, Kenneth Vaughn, 1920–
Crawford, Ken
    Listening to Mother Nature in West Virginia / Ken Crawford
    1st ed.
        p. cm.
    I. Title   CIP:

ISBN: 1-59872-050-3
Printed in the United States of America.

COVER PHOTO:
© 1963 by Ken Crawford
View of the Potomac River and the hamlet of Great Cacapon:
2.5 miles **east of Great Cacapon** and 2.5 miles **west of Berkeley Springs,** in Morgan County.

ILLUSTRATIONS:
Autumn Leaves © 2005 by Tracy Herrmann

To my sisters' children
and their families
who live in Virginia and West Virginia.

Kenneth V. Crawford
Paw Paw High School Graduate, 1938

Acknowledgment

*To my teacher at Paw Paw High School,
Morgan County, West Virginia.*

Thank you, Miss Bell.

*Your decision to leave Chicago and to teach high school
in West Virginia made a difference in my life.*

PREFACE

Although I wrote a lot of poems as a teenager, I wrote even more in my middle-age years – often capturing what it was like for me to grow up in West Virginia.

A strange thing happens when people get to middle age. They seem to lose their grasp on life; they seem to be teenagers again – not knowing who they are, where they are, or where they're going. What makes this span in life serious is the fact that, unlike teenagers, middle-agers don't have a lifetime left to solve their problems, and they know it.

Having traveled a lot in my lifetime and having lived close to Mother Nature in California for 60 years, my heart is still in West Virginia . . . a long ways away . . .

Nevertheless, for a life of love, satisfaction, devotion, faith, and – yes – pleasure in being alive, I want to thank both "mommy and pappy" and Mother Nature.

Ken Crawford

KEN CRAWFORD

To contact Mr. Crawford,
send email messages care of his daughter,
Anjali Crawford:

~~anjalic@earthlink.net~~
ajctravels@yahoo.com
Re: Ken's poetry book

CONTENTS

LISTENING

I must say to myself,
be still
be still
be still,
else I cannot hear
the gentle wind of spring,
caressing the bony limbs
of winter.

Silence, you ravenous mind,
be still
be still
be still,
else I cannot hear the
quiet yawn of the Redwood,
slumbering from heat
in the afternoon.

I must listen quietly, carefully,
be still
be still
be still,
else I cannot sense the life
that made the tree;
naked, dead it stands
in its watery bier
pale shadow to awakening stars.

Quiet, greedy Mind, that Heart may hear
be still
be still
be still,
else I shall waste the mountain top,
and fail to see the sunset
with my heart,
or miss the dawn – conceived
at twilight's
coolness.

July 14, 1974

1

There is this town,*
its clapboards peeling,
grubby,
    dingy,
        streets,
but red lights stop the crossing,
where old men sit and rock;
young dreams they dream,
that's all
    they
       got,
to fit between the nods
and dozes;
they wait for God to talk,
at sunset when the
moon
    comes
       up.
But moonlight is dim and
they don't hear too well,
when
    God
      talks,
keep waiting for the light
to go to green; young dreams
(to walk the streets)
to
    become
       reality.
But no one stands at the corner
under the light;
they say to dream is life, or to
live
    is
      dreams:
won't matter much
when
    God
      talks.

July 7, 1975
*Great Cacapon, West Virginia

THOUGHTS

of stones that groan when
    frost breaks them.
of trees that splinter when
    lightening strikes them.
of brooks that sing when
    water fills them.
of children that cry when
    bees sting them.
of lovers that lie when
    love leaves them.
of frightened mice when
    cats catch them.
of babies that doze when
    mothers nurse them.
of people's dreams when
    love captures them.
of men's souls that live when
    life leaves them.

April 1973

Dawn,
just the coming
of
day?

Dawn,
just the perfectedness
of mountain,
of sun?

Dawn,
its beauty lies within,
the mists,
the stillness.

Dawn,
the mystique of light,
colour,
promise.

April 15, 1975

April's tender leaves a-straining
tell me spring is fast a-gaining.
They snatch a bit of Apollo's fire,
to tease the dragon from his lair.
Swathing their loins in summer rain,
they seek the battle that's to be fought,
never knowing it will come to naught.

When winter sends an icy blast
to rob them of their sweet repast,
they'll lose their will to stiffened sinews
and sense Apollo's cryptic clues.
When greens to reds to browns are changing,
I'll not easily forget; they were a-budding
when they were so (very new). . .

Spring 1976

5

Today I am not alone.
I walk the field, the hills
            along the brooks.
Today I felt the warmth
of nest where frightened
            rabbit fled.
Today I am not alone;
whispers of the woodman's
            saw I hear.
Today a snowflake for
a brief respite, lay upon
            my hand.
Today I am not alone,
for rain in silent splendor
            falls.
Today I live with a
rainbow arched across
            the sky.
Today I am not alone;
laughter wells within my
            throat.
Today the Earth lives
and I loved and was
            loved.
Today I am at peace
with self and I am
            not alone.

November 6, 1972

FRIEND

When I know you
as a friend,
I unlock my chest
of treasures,
to make a place for you.
A place amongst
the laughter,
the tears,
the loves
of my youth.
You stand with me in the
misty dawn
of our newness.
You share
the dew-filled webs
that appear with the sun
of the morning.
You're part of all that
I am.
You share my secret places.
You add
your laughter,
your tears,
your love,
to a treasure that now belongs
to
us.

April 20, 1975

COMPTON'S POND*

Under the sycamore
our voices.
Compton's pond docile
waiting.
Cool cloth for sweating
skins.
Charles, Bob, Benny
and I.
For a moment bare toes
tease the coolness.
Ripples spend their
strength on yonder
bank.
Dragon flies, water skippers,
brave hot sunlight
seeking new
shade.
Thunder rattles on
yonder ridge, through
the sycamore.
Quiet almost reverent,
bare bodies poise on
muddy bank.
Seeing each other,
knowing what
we are.
A dove calls beyond
the sycamore.
We are part of it,
new breast of life;
we nurse it.
Feeling wicked and bold
we plunge in the stream.

May 1965
Revised March 8, 1973

*Compton's Pond: a calm, smooth flow of the Cacapon
River, south of the steel-girder bridge on Route 9.

Small miracle snuggled
in her blanket
of stars.
Conception forced into
being by infinity's
love.
The face of her, pleasant,
beautiful, perfect
she is.
Perfect to the moss-coated
stones of her
brooks.
If I am part of her, she
loves me none
the less.
Could it be that I
am she and she
is I?
If that be true, what
part of she
am I?
And what part
of I
is she?
Why is my soul torn,
when I think
of her?
I don't know,
but she bore me;
I love her.
Earth and I,
the sweat of His hands,
He loves.

January 21, 1974

If you must,
Rampage,
you river of madness,
strip the delicate moss,
with vulgar, wickedness,
from my splendid, silent stones.
Rip through the stagnant
pools:
the algae choked tranquility.
yet
the rain came so softly
I felt only the wetness;
the promise
counted the sheaves of its harvest
how I waited for its ripening.
yet
I know one drop
of softly falling rain
dares not to dream,
such an impudent dream.
What
billion cells within me
changed the wetness to a river.
Swift, Surging, Powerful
stripping the tender living moss
from my
        Splendid
            silent
               stones...

April 1980

STUMP-WATER

When your granite ramparts
lay in alluvial rubble
at
    your
        feet;

and your well-tended blossoms
lay scorched and wilted,
beaten
        to the
            Earth;

and the sweet perfume of life
becomes a rancid odor,
inundating
        your
            nostrils.

Why not laugh a bit,

or cry awhile,

or perhaps you could
suck your idle thumb.

How am i to know
where
    your
        heart is.

August 21, 1975

ROAD RIDGE (a one-room school)

so what did I learn
at road ridge:
i can write (can't i?)
telling you about, the tea berries,
growin' by the woods' path
to Willet's Run Holler,*
how to follow a rabbit track
in a skiff of snow.
(to cipher)
and
wear a dunce cap (with dignity).
learned about girls,
from the (old) boys;
(found out later) they didn't know much.
my punishment place:
the knee hole of Miss Zinn's desk;
giggles, laughter,
but
she smelled good.
the cool water from the pump,
under a great oak;
the pungent odors
of wet wool, bodies,
in the cloak room.
learned how to shoot marbles (too)
(for keeps).
seemed of great importance then.
i learned to weave (the fantasy)
into the reality;
you can hardly tell one, from t'other.
i can't either.

May 11, 1985
*Run Holler: a small creek that is sometimes wet and often very dry

Note: Miss Zinn was the maiden name of Mrs. Margaret Daly
of Great Cacapon.

BRIAR BOTTOM

Once massive virgin oaks
sought the sun to grow,
listening to the stealthy
feet of time so long ago.
Frivolous squirrels raced
the limbs, stinting the quietness.
Echoes of the woodman's ax,
whisperings of his saw.
A sound: a knell of death
they could not know.
Why count the rings of
fresh-cut stumps,
when arteries to the sun are gone?
No matter how old they are:
they are no longer.
No ear to catch the whispering
wind or leaf to mourn
frosts touching.
No boughs from whence
the eagle sought
the cobalt skies:
or sat to rest.
Greenbriers cloak the
biers: rotted stumps
of planks that hold
the pigs in sty;
of ships that ply the sea
and wait to die.

April 1, 1973

The Stag was slain,
froth of fright
upon his
nostrils.
Was slain,
and the chase did end:
his throbbing body
hot upon the
Earth.
Was slain,
his warmth,
his life,
now red torrent
poured upon
the frozen
Earth.
Was slain,
and the Earth
cared not
at all.
Was slain,
no more to quaff
the honey-wine
of springtime.
Was slain,
no more to scrape the velvet,
or nibble on the tender
shoots,
or rut,
when rutting season comes.
Was slain,
and my heart convulsed
within my breast,
For I was not
hungry . . .

May 17, 1974

THE STONE

The stone
gives of itself,
that a
brook might have a song.
The brook
then sings about the stone,
that it (had need of).
The Earth,
is happy that they sing.

The lovers
say aloud: I do;
I give myself to you.

(I do)
seems such a small thing
but
myself is all I have to give...

March 25, 1976

MY STONE

The stone, part of life and light
and all that is
or was.
I feel its many days of brightness,
sense the eons of
its darkness:
coolness on my
fingertips.
The stone wearied,
by roots,
by winter,
also knows the spring,
warmth, sun,
petals that touch
with love,
its crusty face.
I stand awhile in dusty river beds,
that once in raging torrents
fled its being.
Where are the rivers
that shaped my
stone?
Where does the light shine
that it was
part of?
Or am I a dreamer,
awakened in the misty dawn
and only think I
know the
stone?

But the sun is warm when morning comes:
and
my thoughts they flee
from feelings
ferment,
for with my heart
I feel the texture of
my stone,
and know the life
within – it.

April 16, 1974

SKINNY DIPPING

I met
this slender girl,
sitting
naked
on my stone.
How could she be there
with
her shiny, wet skin
and
her eyes of mystery?
Shall I
throw her off my throne
or
shuck my clothes
and share that stone?
She
waited,
a saucy smile within her eyes,
until
my butt
was firmly
on the stone.
Then,
she cast a rainbow of awe
around me.
For the span of
a candle's flicker,
a
woman
sat beside me.
Laughter
mingled with our shyness,
as
wet
butts
shivered on our stone.

May 28, 1975

THE SWINGING BRIDGE

Mystical path, ecstasy
of youth.
Its cables rusted, failing
with age.
Its pathway weathered,
splintered, worn.
It felt the laughter of
happy feet.
Quivered, swayed under
fearful hearts.
One special day we
walked the bridge.
Hands, hearts holding
the moments.
Love caught us up
walking its boards.
We savored the zephyrs
of life within us.
Was it built just for
us that day?
A kiss for the tears as
we gained the gate.
Today no fingers grip
its cables.
No hearts tremble on
its span.
Tears no longer dampen
its boards.
No kiss as I gain the
gate.

March 1973

THE GLEN

We dreamed our way
along the path,
crossing the talking
brook at last.

Our brook, it had
a few words to say:
"You seek for love,
in my sunny, spring day."

Spring was on the earth
and love beckoned to us.
Its energy, its being,
teased a new aware-ness.

On the lush spring grass
in the sun-warmed glen,
suddenly there were lovers
where once there were friends.

March 21, 1975

TO A LEAF

What does one say
to a fallen leaf?
That it's good to lay there
because you were alive?
That time through winter's
door has come to call?
Remember the summer
when life surged
strong within you?
Your course is finished
and you have won?
Nay, fallen warrior,
your weapons are gone,
your battle is done,
You have fallen
with your colours;
beautiful as they are,
they cannot save you.

October 30, 1972

*In memory of my father, Elmer Crawford, who died in 1972
at home in Great Cacapon, West Virginia.*

BACK YONDER

Back yonder,
when we were children,
Pappy sowed the
turnip seeds,
in the brown Earth
after the potatoes
were dug
up.
I remember,
I didn't like turnips,
except when the frost pushed
them out of the
Earth.
They were crisp and cold then,
from the frost,
not tasting like turnips
ought to taste,
and I was hungry then.
I remember,
Pappy sowing the turnips,
walking the brown Earth,
looking to me.
He has left,
but I don't sow the turnip seeds,
for there is no one
to eat them,
when the frost pushes
them out of the
Earth.

September 27, 1974

In memory of my father, Elmer Crawford.

Before September,
the grass already dry
upon the hills,
dust of the summer
thick on weedy paths.
The hawk languid in
dwindling sky,
high above the canyon's
blanket of heat.

Before September,
we gain the mountain-top;
sleep on September, awaken not.
It's cold as evening spreads
its gentle colour upon us,
and September's caught up
within the coolness of it.
Clean air to breathe, God to see,
and no dust upon our leaves.

Before September,
summer lay in the valley,
far below our beating hearts,
and we felt the mountain
alive beneath our feet,
shivered in the glory
that we are part of.
Mists of the mountain,
we embrace your coolness.

Before September,
a day we have known dies,
that Night be born from it.
But our hearts are not
with the knowing of it,
for on the wings of Morning,
a new day awaits us.
A day to walk in, to love in,
before September comes.

August 17, 1974

SMELLS LIKE "PUNKIN" TIME*

I mark the time by Punkin clocks
but old man Sol still has a say.
The chill of his shadows they pimple me
but he'll burn my head (come day).

Ol' Sol can feel the chill at his heels
and sees the frost colour his leaves.
'Tis a pity he cries to the winter wind
but the wind has no ear, to hear his pleas.

His laughter rings o'er the frozen brooks;
they try to sing but their music's gone.
And he'll not tell them anything
(they can sing again) when spring has come.

(Punkins must come), (Punkins must go),
and we all must (bide our time) at the gate.
Except ol' Sol, he don't need a Punkin clock
and I need not worry that he'll be late.

September 24, 1975

*In West Virginia, "pumpkin" is pronounced "punkin."

THE CREEK

Leaves, programmed to fall,
chill winds will come
to strew their colours about;
seems an absolute law.

They are dry now,
a very lifeless state,
skittering on cold stones;
(les finis) a final bow.

Time snatched the leaves,
colouring their final glory,
leaving trees cold naked;
it's time (now) to grieve.

It's me (here) just me,
here at the creek,
scanning banks (cold-bare)
as far as I can see.

November 20, 1983

WHY CRY YE?

Turbid driven dust of
               earth.
Sorrow rampant laughter
               durst.
Ye sour the face of
               earth.
Vain peacock strutting
               forth.
Sensual creation stalking
               earth.
Ye fear the night and
               curse.
Aimless ye spoil the face of
               earth.
Pile high ye shifting dunes of
               dust.
Night comes, oh dust of
               earth.
Ye fragments of God's
               birth.
Ye infants nurse the breast of
               earth.
Twilight, velvet warmth, day
               burst.
The rain will come, dust of
               earth.

January 23, 1973

! DAWN !

Just the advent of day.
Prosaic, ordinary,
change from darkness.
Misty promises in warmth
of first love's
kiss.
Budding young breasts
striving for midday,
to suckle in
brightness.
Another stone, building day's
pyramid from rubble of
darkness.
Love's artesian
flow from
unmeasured wells
of spirit.
Ignorance;
Warrior of the night,
jousted, wounded mortally,
by knowing.
Day awaits bold user,
dawn the threshold
to it.
Death strikes from faceless
clocks;
Faint flicker of light?
!Dawn!

October 1973

27

Love has existence
in the embrace that Earth
with candid ecstasy bestows
upon her ancient Oaks,
offering her distended breast;
though probing hungry roots,
seek to violate her being.

Would there be no breast
unless there is an Oak?
Me-thinks the Earth would
create a mighty Oak,
just to end her spinster-hood
and revel in conjugal feeling.
Because she (is) the Earth.

March 17, 1976

LITTLE ACORN

You think you shall be
a great oak?
Will moss grow on your
gnarled trunk?
Will birds nest the crotch of
your branches?
Will squirrels store your
fruit for winter's season?
Will frost drop your
leaves for a carpet?
Will spring finding you
leafless, nurse you?
Shall man fell your
trunk for his shelter?
Little acorn, how do you
know to be a great oak?

September 30, 1973

DEATH OF A SQUIRREL

Through forest cold
The hunter strides;
Home and hearth
Are thrust aside;
The night gives way
To sun and sky.
The hunter man
Crouches slowly down,
To await Mr. Squirrel
As he makes his rounds.
Plump nuts await
On lofty boughs;
For Mr. Squirrel
They do abound.
Frenzied – barking
Heralds the dawn
As nuts from lofty
Boughs are shorn.
Man hunter slowly
Aims his gun,
Pulls the trigger,
Snuffs out the fun.
In the fullness of life
He was oblivious of death.
Nuts forgotten forever
On the winter's ground.

February 1965

Careful as you walk
the Earth!

That your feet not
leave a tadpole
crushed.

That your hands not
strip the ivy from
a wall.

That your knee not
leave a slender daisy
broken.

That in climbing the tree
the fruit is left
to ripen.

That in viewing tiny birds
the mother is not
frightened.

That the mouse not be
trapped without
reason.

That the hunter not
become the
hunted.

That a friend not
be left without
shelter.

Be careful;
they all bruise as easily as
you or I.

August 1973

MAN'S KNOWLEDGE

Man must know
the reasons why
babes are born
and some must die;
why chill winds blow
and leaves must fall,
he reasons why.

He'll stare to see
whence comes the tide,
and stand in awe,
when kittens nurse;
or seek to answer
his loneliness,
he reasons why.

He probes the sea,
the earth and sky;
the stars – they seem
to mystify.
He seeks out love
and hopes to know
the reasons why.

As evening sun
paints the sky,
he waits for dawn
and another try.
While dewdrops shimmer
against the sky,
he reasons why.

The need for work
and his need to play;
he wonders why
he needs to pray;
and to what god
on this bright day?
he reasons why.

Within the shadowed
depth of mind
there stirs a fetal consciousness.
That reason is the soul of man;
its dusty corners cry to know
the reason why.

Man seeks to know
the reasons why;
he seldom seeks
the why of Reason.

August 31, 1972

EARTHMAN

With wonder I view:
    the tumbling cataracts of thought,
    sculptors of the mind.
With wonder I view:
    my heart beating, with life, love,
    hearthstones of being.
With wonder I view:
    the limpid pools of the Spirit,
    bathing my Soul.
With wonder I view:
    the turbulent, vivid, travellings
    of my being.
With wonder I view:
    the lowly snail as he spreads his footprint
    of slime.
With wonder I view:
    licentious moonlight stalking silently;
    forests of the innocent.
With wonder I view:
    seeding of brown meadows;
    harvests that will come.
With wonder I view:
    my mountains tall, while sweating to climb
    the ramparts to them.
With wonder I view:
    my years break their moorings;
    sliding into antiquity's sea.
With wonder I view:
    my steaming geysers of feeling;
    erupting from within my being.
With wonder I view:
    men weeping for yesterday,
    wishing for tomorrow, not living today.
With wonder I view:
    that which I am; that which I am not;
    wondering what can I be.

August 1973

LIVING IT

I woke up this morning
feeling down,
seemed like God
walked on me;
with
dirty
feet.
Then I saw the sun
light up the frost,
on my
fence post;
and I
wasn't
down.
God don't walk on people
with dirty feet,
I only thought he did,
because I think like me;
not
like
him.
When morning quits coming
for me,
I can be God,
or frost
on
a
fence post,
or whatever
I want to be.

December 4, 1974

RAPE OF A RAINBOW

I build my castles
with stones of love
and stack my selfish bricks
(up high)
and paint with white,
my palings fair.
A fief-dom i build
with nary a care.
Then speculate (i)
on the when and where.
I know he waits (quietly)
beyond fief-dom's wall,
(churlish) Black Knight,
astride his mount so tall.
(Someday)
a lightening swift blow
of his glistening sword
will sever my rainbow,
from its pot of Gold.

December 30, 1975

THING CALLED MAN

The flotsam vomit
of primordial sea?
Growth from alluvial
mass of creation?
A complexity of mind
embodied in flesh?
Striving to stand in
a quagmire of life
not knowing quite how
or why he must.
He thinks – so he is;
he is – so he thinks.
He's a part of the swift
river of life whose
headwaters were formed
in the mountains of creation;
Its roily waters tearing
at channel and banks,
plunging ever onward
in its race to the Sea.
The spirit of man,
an island of light
firm in the midst
of the swift river of life.
With pristine consciousness
searches for truth.
The spirit of man
searching for God
not knowing – IT IS.

December 1965
Revised October 1972

CHALICE

A part of myself (lonely)
while striding through hell,
strains ears to listen
for the ring of the bells.
That clear articulate pealing I hear
that talks of love.

Their song is in the swift
flight of the swallows
and I see the shape of them
in the mist-filled hollows.
My heart (it tells me) that
not I (alone) know love.

I sense their naked clarity
in the screaming storm
and I feel their tender heart
when the sun is warm.
Then dare (i) again to cry
aloud that (all is love).

Days walk hard upon me
but they hardly seem to gain,
so long as I can hear
'bells' in the summer rain,
or wet my thirsting soul with
a draught* from the cup of love.

September 20, 1975

*Old English word that means a "drink," pronounced "droth."

LOVE, WHENCE COME YOU?

And who could see
the hurricane in
a patch of
clouds?
Did the sprouting seed
know its roots
could split a
stone?
Was not the tinder
willing for fire to
burn it?
The love's fire storm,
searing the weeds and
grass of the dry
places.
Lighting the dark places,
scouring the canyons,
racing to the high
places.
Driving the living things
in awe before its
power.
Making our minds, our
bodies, a captive of
its being.
Lapping of the coolness
at the brooks along
its pathways.
When its energy is
spent, gentleness
comes.
Then slumbering quietly,
listless, dreams of new
awakening.

Love, whence come you?

January 4, 1974

MAN'S TIME

A measured fragment
of God's infinity.
A thing to use
in its increments.

Measured by laughter
anguish and tears.
Measured by hours
and a billion light years.

Created in conscious
mind of man;
Elusive vapor tenuous
in sleep and death.

Transcending our hopes,
our dreams and fears.
What shall we do
with its slippery years?

Shall hours be love
and minutes be tears,
as we measure our
lives over the years?

By chance I received
this brief span of time,
that cannot exist
except in my mind.

Times for me alone
to curse the darkness,
or cheer the light
within my consciousness.

In the sweeping curve
of my God's infinity,
shall time's small segment
for me mean love?

January 1972

MAN'S LOVE

Expression of love
Takes many forms.
It starts the day
That we are born.

Its many devious
Channels – formed,
Oft by chance
And conscience-born.

It bends our will
And drives our lives,
As down the hill
Of life we slide.

Quick to turn
To hate and fear,
As passion burns
Upon our ears.

Sometimes as soft
As ducklings' down,
And yet as rough
As an ancient frown.

Man thinks he knows
From whence it came,
But using it now
Becomes his game.

To know the joys
Of love returned,
Is not a ploy
That we can earn.

Our just reward
For sharing soul,
Is love's accord
With a kindred soul.

December 15, 1971

MY LOVE

Bold upon the ridge,
free of tangled brush,
branches merge with
sky.
Grasping the wind,
knowing the sun,
you will not
die.
Your crystal streams
in narrow canyons flow;
high cliffs they mingle
with your song;

Your gentle breeze,
blowing before
the rains that quench
your thirsty
roots.
You flower before the seed
or leaf that falls
upon the Earth
that bear
you.

There is no spring, no planting,
no beginning or end,
existing before I;
you were.

My love not something
I understand;
Something that I am
or am not.

December 1973

ALPHA IS LOVE

And
we shall walk on
the
pinnacles of the cosmos
and
we shall know love
and we shall know beauty
and
you shall know (I am)
and
you shall be part of me again;
wholly,
as we were (at beginning)
and
love shall create oneness,
where estrangement existed
and
this
oneness in love, beauty,
shall
become part of all that is:
(again)
          forever ... (I promise.)

March 20, 1977

Appendix

HAPPY BIRTHDAY

Forty: no serious blow.
Having passed 20 twice
In the game of life,
You are now at Go!

A FEW WEST VIRGINIA SAYINGS:

- Don't throw the baby out with the bath water.
- That's as long as a well rope.

Regarding friendships and relationships:
- Why pull the hair of the dog that bit you?!
- No one pulls my string (latch string) unless I let them.

To men and their future mother-in-laws:
- You have to pet the cow before you can have the calf.

Created by Ken Crawford:
- Why keep a dog if you do all the barking yourself?
- Man doesn't grow into eternity; he is born into it.

Regarding poverty and health:
- He's as poor as Job's turkey; he has to lean on the fence to gobble.

Regarding the weather:
- It's colder than a witch's nose!   (originally: "a witch's tit")
- Hotter than the hubs of hell.
- It's raining cats and dogs.

Often used by Ken's mother, Fanny Crawford:
- When it rains and the sun shines, the devil is whipping his wife.

Springtime and sexual drive:
- Wild as a March hare.

About the Author . . .

Kenneth Vaughn Crawford was born in 1920 in Great Cacapon, where he roamed among the hills, mountains, forests, valleys, and rivers of wonderful West Virginia.

He grew up with four sisters and no brothers. In the summer of 1928, he and one of his sisters nearly died of typhoid fever after drinking creek water.

Ken's love of both reading and writing poetry started at a very young age. He truly enjoyed reading English literature. Often he would daydream about *King Arthur and the Round Table.*

Because his parents saw the value of education, he was given the opportunity to finish high school in Paw Paw of Morgan County. Although the bus ride required one hour in each direction, Ken enjoyed this time of reading, day-dreaming, and writing poetry.

A few years later, he was caught up in World War II and served two years in the South Pacific as a hospital corpsman. Upon returning to the U.S., in 1944, he married an Italian woman, whom he had met on leave in San José, California, in 1942. Thus, he had chosen a new adventure in California, and a few years later, he had two daughters, a lovely home, and a steady job. He worked for 35 years as a master mechanic at a large chemical plant.

Friendships, with many people, and his life in the Appalachian Mountains have lent themselves in so many ways to Ken Crawford's poetry. Although he has lived in California for more than 60 years, his "home" in West Virginia is never far away.

ORDER POETRY BOOKS
BY KEN CRAWFORD

~ ~ ~

Listening to Mother Nature in West Virginia
40 poems

::

Knowing the Wind
100 poems
includes all poems printed in
Listening to Mother Nature in West Virginia

~ ~ ~

For current price information (including shipping), write to:

Anjali Crawford
Publisher and Distributor
~~anjalic@earthlink.net~~ - *or* - ajctravels@yahoo.com
RE: Poetry Book Order

- Book title(s).
- How many.
- Your name and postal mailing address.
- Your phone number.

Or fax your request to: 1-510-652-0501.
No phone calls, please; the direct fax-line is available 24 hours a day.
Be sure to include *your phone number* and *address.*

Or visit **Anjali Online** and fill out an order form:
http://home.earthlink.net/~anjalic/orderbooks.html

Thank you!